...GRASS IN THE SKY

THE BOOK OF
CLOUGH

OLD BIG 'EAD
IN HIS OWN WORDS

> **"** If God had wanted us to play football in the clouds,
> he'd have put grass in the sky. **"**

Copyright © 2005 Naked Guides Limited.

Publishers: Steve Faragher, Richard Jones.

Design: Joe Burt.

ISBN 0-9544177-2-0
The first moral right of the author has been asserted.

First published in Great Britain in 2005 by Toilet Books, an imprint of
Naked Guides Limited, The Studio, Little Theatre Cinema, Bath BA1 1SF.

Front cover and title page pictures supplied by Colorsport.

Typeset in Myriad Pro and Broken 15. Broken 15 was created by Eduardo Recife.
Visit his website at www.misprintedtype.com

Thanks to Nigel Clough and Nick Moyle.

Collected by **Alex Murphy**

This book is dedicated to the memory of
Brian Clough (1935-2004)

Contents

Brian Clough's Career Statistics

Born: Grove Hill, Middlesbrough, 21st March 1935
Died: Derby City Hospital, 20th September 2004

As a player

Club	Year	Appearances	Goals
Middlesbrough	1953-61	213	197
Sunderland	1961-65	61	54
Total		**274**	**251**
England	1959	2	0

England appearances

England vs Wales, Ninian Park, Cardiff, 17th Oct 1959. British Championship match: Wales 1 England 1.
England vs Sweden, Empire Stadium, Wembley 28th Oct 1959. Friendly: England 2 Sweden 3.

As a manager

Club	Year	Games	Won	Lost	Drawn
Hartlepool Utd	1965-67	84	35	36	13
Derby County	1967-73	289	135	84	70
Brighton	1973-74	32	12	12	8
Leeds Utd	1974	7	1	3	3
Nottingham Forest	1975-93	907	411	250	246
Total		**1319**	**594**	**385**	**340**

Club honours

DERBY COUNTY

1968/69: *Football League Division Two champions*

1970/71: *Watney Cup winners*

1971/72: *Football League champions, Texaco Cup winners*

LEEDS UNITED

1974/75: *FA Charity Shield runners-up*

NOTTINGHAM FOREST

1976/77: *Anglo-Scottish Cup winners*

1977/78: *Football League champions, League Cup winners*

1978/79: *European Cup winners, League Cup winners, FA Charity Shield winners, Football League runners-up*

1979/80: *European Cup winners, League Cup runners-up, European Super Cup winners, Football League runners-up*

1980/81: *European Super Cup runners-up*

1988/89: *League Cup winners, Simod Cup winners*

1989/90: *League Cup winners*

1990/91: *FA Cup runners-up*

1991-92: *League Cup runners-up, Zenith Data Systems Cup winners*

Individual honours

1978: *Manager of the Year*

1992: *PFA Merit Award*

Distinctions: Received an O.B.E. in 1991.

The Book of Clough

BRIAN CLOUGH is the greatest football manager England has ever produced.

His reputation as one of the legends of the game would have been secure even if his career had ended after his spell as **Derby County manager**. After all, to turn just one shambolic east Midlands outfit into the Champions of England would have been a great achievement in itself. But his Baseball Ground interlude was just the warm up for one of the most astonishing feats of management the world has ever seen, let alone this country.

Clough took over at County's neighbours, **Nottingham Forest**, in 1975. He inherited a depressed Second Division club going nowhere. By sheer force of will Clough took them up into the First Division, won the Championship the year after, and for an encore inspired a team sprinkled with has-beens and never-weres to become Champions of Europe. Then he did it all over again.

Nothing he did in his career thereafter could match that – but then how could it?

Clough was famous for far more than just the exploits of his teams. His personality and gift for coining a memorable phrase made him a **household name** even in non-football households who thought Nottingham Forest was a beauty spot just off the M1.

It would be an exaggeration to say he was universally loved – he was never the nation's favourite uncle. After all, he was variously described as conceited, big-headed, bullying, boastful, **opinionated and loud** – and that was by Clough himself.

Clough was in his pomp in the late Seventies and although he would never have associated himself with the roots of **punk rock**, he represented many of the values that were sweeping through youth culture and music – he was a rebel, he often clashed with authority and he had utter self belief. The following pages record some of the man's most outrageous claims, quips and remarks both cruel and kind. They stand as an eloquent tribute to a person who always had something to say, and someone who was always worth hearing.

6

Picture: *Clough in contemplative mood at Nottingham Forest. (Colorsport)*

ModEsty

" I wouldn't say I was the best manager in the business. But I was in the top one. **"**

" They say Rome wasn't built in a day, but I wasn't on that particular job. **"**

" I am a big head not a figurehead. **"**

ArroganCe

" On occasions I have been big-headed. I think most people are when they get in the limelight. I call myself Big Head just to remind myself not to be. **"**

" I said to him, you'll have to widen the hospital doors if you and I walk in together, because they won't get both heads through one door. **"**

To the liver transplant surgeon who told Clough he was the best surgeon in the country.

KnowleDge

" Age does not count. It's what you know about football that matters. I know I am better than the 500 or so managers who have been sacked since the war. If they had known anything about the game, they wouldn't have lost their jobs. "

MiraCles

" It's easy enough to get to Ireland – just a walk across the Irish Sea as far as I'm concerned. **"**

Cloughie chases Jack Charlton's old job.

" The river Trent is lovely. I know because I have walked on it for 18 years. **"**

WaLes

" I can't promise to give the team talks in Welsh, but from now on I'll be taking my holidays in Porthcawl and I've bought a complete set of Harry Secombe albums. **"**

Cloughie sets his sights on the Wales job.

PigeOns

" The pigeons in Derby will welcome the news. There'll be more room on my head to shit on than anyone else. "

Cloughie's reaction to plans for a statue in his honour in Derby.

MortaLity

❝ Success? Tell me the date when my obituary is going to appear and I'll tell you whether I've been a success or not. If I get to 60 I shall have done pretty well. **❞**

❝ I want no epitaphs of profound history and all that type of thing. I contributed. I would hope they would say that, and I would hope somebody liked me. **❞**

❝ When I go, God's going to have to give up his favourite chair. **❞**

ResigNation

" Resignations are for Prime Ministers and those caught with their trousers down, not for me. "

KnEes

" I think my knees have got worse. I'll have to order a new pair from the Co-op for Christmas. I am all right sitting down or in bed, but if I get in a car they lock. The bloke who said life begins at 40 was either blind drunk or in cloud-cuckoo land. There is only one way to go when you're 40 – down. **"**

TeA

❝ I'm ill-tempered, rude and wondering what's for tea. Just the same as always. **❞**

In retirement Cloughie explains what he gets up to at a quarter to five on a Saturday.

Trousers

❝ I might be an old codger now and slightly past my best as a gaffer, but the FA would know they're safe with me. At least I'd keep my trousers on. **❞**

RetiRement

" I've decided to pick my moment to retire very carefully – in about 200 years time. **"**

AlcOhol

" Walk on water? I know most people out there will be saying that instead of walking on it, I should have taken more of it with my drinks. They are absolutely right. **"**

" I'm dealing with my drinking problem and I have a reputation for getting things done. **"**

PreSsUre

" I knew I was the best but I should have said nowt and kept the pressure off 'cos they'd have worked it out for themselves. **"**

22

on The BeaUtiful gaMe

Picture: *Cloughie scores for Middlesbrough in a 1957 FA Cup replay victory over Charlton Athletic. (Empics)*

GOaLs

❝ It only takes a second to score a goal. **❞**

Cloughie the TV pundit during England's World Cup qualifier against Poland at Wembley in 1973.

BirtH

" Doing well in football is like childbirth. It doesn't happen overnight. **"**

RoaSt beeF

" You don't want roast beef and Yorkshire every night and twice on Sunday. "

Cloughie warns on the game's over-exposure on TV.

VictOry

" I gave my players a version of the same message at ten-to-three
every Saturday: 'I would shoot my granny right now for three
points this afternoon.' They knew how important it was to give
everything in the cause of victory. Every time. That's why
my granny enjoyed more lives than my cat. **"**

Tactics

" Players lose you games, not tactics. There's so much crap talked about tactics by people who barely know how to win at dominoes. **"**
On England's exit from Euro 2000.

ReFereeS

" It was a crooked match and he was a crooked referee. That was a tournament we could and should have won. **"**

On the 1984 UEFA Cup Semi-Final Forest lost to Anderlecht.

BaLLs

❝ I can't even spell spaghetti never mind talk Italian. How could I tell an Italian to get the ball? He might grab mine. **❞**

On the influx of foreign players into English football.

MorE baLLs

" Learn to play first, then you can have as many match balls as you like. **"**

Peter Withe asks Cloughie for the match ball after scoring four goals for Nottingham Forest.

Picture: *Clough with Peter Taylor at their testimonial match between Forest and Derby in 1978. (Empics)*

PeteR Taylor

" I've missed him. He used to make me laugh. He was the best diffuser of a situation I have ever known. I hope he's all right. **"**

" I'm not equipped to manage successfully without him. I'm the shop front, he is the goods at the back. **"**

" We pass each other on the A52 going to work on most days of the week. But if his car broke down and I saw him thumbing a lift, I wouldn't pick him up, I'd run him over. **"**

On the man who was Clough's Lieutenant at Brighton, Forest and Derby after Taylor left to manage Derby on his own.

NelSOn MandeLa

" I hope you were as delighted as I was last week when Nelson Mandela was freed from a South African jail. But what I hadn't bargained for was that his release was going to cut across the start of our Littlewoods Cup final. **"**

Sir Alex Ferguson

" For all his horses, knighthoods and championships, he hasn't got two of what I've got. And I don't mean balls. "

Double European Cup-winner Cloughie puts Sir Alex in his place.

JoSe Mourinho

" I like the look of Mourinho, there's a bit of the young Clough about him. **"**

Brian Clough shortly before his death.

BarbAra ClOugh

" Barbara's supervising the move. She's having more extensions built than Heathrow airport. **"**

Cloughie delegates the important decisions to Mrs Clough

" We used to go to the pictures every Saturday night but we had to leave a little bit early and get home and watch Match of the Day – and my wife still complains she missed the last five minutes of every film we saw. **"**

On the 40th anniversary of Match of the Day.

NigeL CloUgh

❝ He's not joining Pisa for the simple and most important reason that his mother decided that days ago. **❞**

Nigel misses a dream move to Italy.

MartiN O'NeiLL

❝ Anybody who can do anything in Leicester but make a jumper has got to be a genius. **❞**

❝ If he'd been English or Swedish, he'd have walked the England job. **❞**

Sven-GOran EriksSon.

66 At last England have appointed a manager who speaks English better than the players. 99

Streakers

" The Derby players have seen more of his balls than the one they're meant to be playing with. "

On a streaker who interrupted a Derby County vs Manchester United match.

JimmY HiLL

66 If he can find a ground where he scored a league goal,
I'll meet him there. **99**

On Players

Picture: *Clough with John Robertson after the victory over Liverpool in the 1978 League Cup Final replay. (Empics)*

JoHn RobertTson.

66 He was a very unattractive young man. If I ever felt off colour I'd sit next to him, because compared to this fat, dumpy lad I was Errol Flynn. But give him the ball and a yard of grass and he was an artist. 99

66 He was fatter than I was. But he treated a football better than most people treat a woman. 99

Roy Keane 1

❝ Young Keane shouldn't screw up his privileged position at Old Trafford for the sake of a few thousand extra quid he might make abroad. It's tempting – 60 grand a week after tax and a four year contract. But I reckon that on top of what he has got already, he'd have to live until he's 634 to spend that lot. **❞**

On Keane's prolonged contract negotiations.

❝ I believe Lennox Lewis didn't see that punch coming last Sunday and the skipper of the Titanic had some excuse for not spotting an iceberg if it was dark. But I couldn't believe my big ears when Fergie said he had not seen Keane's tackle on Haaland. **❞**

On selective shortsightedness.

DaviD SeAman

" That Seaman is a handsome young man but he spends too much time looking in his mirror rather than at the ball. You can't keep goal with hair like that. **"**

TreVor BroOking

“ Floats like a butterfly and stings like one too. **”**

KeNny DalgLish

" When he scored he had a better smile than Clark Gable. Beautiful teeth, arms wide, that's how he celebrated. He wasn't that big, but he had a huge arse. It came down below his knees and that's where he got his strength from. "

RoY Keane 2

" I get sick and tired of hearing how much running Keane does. He has had more than enough rest through suspensions alone. He's had more holidays than Judith Chalmers. **"**

" If Keane wants to do that I'll get him a job in a circus. **"**

After Keane celebrated scoring with a somersault.

" I only ever hit Roy the once. He got up so I couldn't have hit him very hard. **"**

KennY BUrns

" Kenny Burns turned up to sign for us in a car without tax or insurance. It's a wonder we weren't arrested. "

Bryan Robson

❝ I wish I was England coach because I'd teach Bryan Robson not to kick and foul people when things go wrong. **❞**

Roy Keane 3

" They say Al Capone did some good things in his life. Trouble was, he would go out in the streets and shoot people. Keane is becoming United's Al Capone. **"**

" Oh, I'd have sent him home alright, but I'd have shot him first. **"**

After Keane's hasty exit from the 2002 World Cup following a verbal attack on Republic of Ireland manager Mick McCarthy.

DaViD BeCKHam

“ Being thick isn't an affliction if you're a footballer because your brains need to be in your feet. Beckham works hard, he's brave and he's a superb crosser. He treats a football like he does his wife – lovingly, with caresses. ”

Steve Hodge

" I haven't just signed a player. I've rescued a lad from hell. **"**

Buying Steve Hodge from Spurs.

PauL GaScoignE

" If we're not careful Paul Gascoigne is going to end up like Matt Monro. Dead before we appreciate his talent. **"**

CoLin TOdd

" He's too expensive. We're not interested. **"**

After being asked about the rumour that he was going to sign
Colin Todd from Sunderland in February 1971. Clough signed Todd that same day.

EriC CantOna

" I'd have cut his balls off. **"**

On Cantona's Kung-Fu Kick

Teddy Sheringham

" When Teddy Sheringham played for me at Nottingham Forest he was the slowest player in the squad – perhaps due to all those nightclubs he kept telling me he didn't frequent. "

FaBieN BartHeZ

" Fabien Barthez looks at times as if he's had more red wine
than I ever managed to drink. **"**

Picture: *Clough and Leeds United players keep their distance before the 1974 Charity Shield against Liverpool. (Empics)*

Leeds United

❝ You got all those medals by cheating. **❞**

To the Leeds United players on his first day as manager.

EnglanD 1

❝ Barbara said I talked myself out of the England job. **❞**

Clough reflects on his forthright interview for the England job.

❝ I don't know who you are and I don't know who gave you permission to come in here – but f*** off. **❞**

Clough to England team doctor Professor Frank O'Gorman when he walked into the youth team dressing room at half time with a plate of oranges.

MiDdlesBrOugh

" The only thing I enjoyed at Middlesbrough was scoring goals. From Saturday to Saturday I was very unhappy. My ability was never utilised. By me or the management. Only goals kept me sane. That was my only pleasure. "

NottInghaM FOresT

❝ Nottingham Forest will never know how lucky they were that they asked me to get on with the job of rebuilding their run-down club. They didn't just need a new manager. The bloody place was so dead it needed the kiss of life. **❞**

❝ Acne is a bigger problem than injuries **❞**

Cloughie puts the accent on youth at Forest.

EngLanD 2

" They didn't want an England manager who was prepared to call the Italians cheating bastards. They failed to understand that I would have curbed my language and revelled in the relief from the day-to-day, month-to-month grind of club management. **"**

" I'll take any job that you care to give me. **"**

Clough's final words to the FA interview panel in 1977. The FA chose Ron Greenwood to manage England and put Clough and Peter Taylor in charge of the England youth team.

ArsenaL

❝ I bet their dressing room will smell of garlic rather than liniment over the next few months. **❞**

On Arsene Wenger's French-dominated Arsenal team.

❝ They caress a football the way I dreamt of caressing Marilyn Monroe. **❞**

On Arsene Wenger's Arsenal

BrightOn & HoVe AlbiOn

" Yes, I remember the Bristol Rovers experience, even though I have tried very hard to forget it! And yes, I also recall not too fondly a non-League side called Walton and Hersham putting me on my backside in an FA Cup replay. The Bristol match was televised and it must have been on the box more times than Coronation Street. Somebody was rejoicing in the fact that Cloughie's team had eight put past them. "

Brighton boss Clough on the televised 8-2 home defeat by Bristol Rovers.

Hartlepool United

❝ People said you could drop off the end of the world if you went there. Sometimes I wished I had. **❞**

EngLand 3

" I'm sure the England selectors thought if they took me on and gave me the job, I'd want to run the show. They were shrewd because that's exactly what I would have done. "

" Bullshit. A Rolls Royce is always a Rolls Royce and it's the same with an England shirt. "

At his interview for the England manager's job in 1977, Clough responds to FA Secretary Ted Croker's suggestion that England should ditch their Admiral shirts.

ManchEster UnITed

" Manchester United in Brazil? I hope they all get bloody diarrhoea. "

On United opting out of the FA Cup to play in the World Club Championship.

on man Management

Picture: *Clough with Kenny Burns and the League Cup after the Final replay victory over Liverpool in 1978. (Colorsport)*

ApPearaNce

" The ugliest player I ever signed was Kenny Burns. "

" Stand up straight, get your shoulders back and get your hair cut. "

Cloughie advises John McGovern at Hartlepool.

AgeNts

❝ If a player had said to Bill Shankly 'I've got to speak to my agent', Bill would have hit him. And I would have held him while he hit him. **❞**

❝ I'm talking to you, not your bimbo. **❞**

To Gary McAllister and his agent.

Selection

" The only person certain of boarding the bus to Wembley for the Littlewoods Cup final is Albert Kershore, and he'll be driving it. "

" I'm as bad a judge of strikers as Walter Winterbottom. He only gave me two caps. "

Colleagues

" I'm fed up with Bobby Robson pointing to his grey hair and saying the England job has aged him ten years. If he doesn't like it why doesn't he go back to his orchard in Suffolk? "

MotiVaTion

66 We talk about it for 20 minutes and then we decide I was right. **99**

On how to deal with uppity players.

66 Don't worry too much about what to do, just give the ball to John Robertson and he'll do the rest… He's a better player than you. **99**

To record £1 million signing Trevor Francis before his first game for Nottingham Forest.

Chairmen 1

“ If a chairman sacks the manager he initially appointed, he should go as well. **”**

“ Of course we discuss the big decisions. We talk about them for a while and he eventually agrees I'm right. **”**

Cloughie on working with his chairman at Forest.

DipLomaCy

" I've found that when things have gone wrong and I've listened to other people's opinions it's been a disaster. The more you listen to people, the more you get off course. **"**

" There are more hooligans in the House of Commons than at a football match. **"**

Coaching

" Coaching is for kids. If a player can't trap a ball and pass it by the time he's in the team he shouldn't be there in the first place. I told Roy McFarland to go out and get his bloody hair cut. That's coaching at top level. "

NeighBours

❝ I thought it was my next-door neighbour because I think she felt that if I got something like that I would have to move. **❞**

Cloughie ponders on who nominated him for a knighthood.

Singing

❝ He should guide Posh in the direction of a singing coach because she's nowhere near as good at her job as her husband. **❞**

❝ Beckham? His wife can't sing and his barber can't cut hair. **❞**

On Posh and Becks.

Chairmen 2

" Football hooligans? Well, there are 92 club chairmen for a start. **"**

" Nowadays chairmen seem to live in Spain. That bloke who was at Forest lived in Monaco. I often wonder how people like that got into football. You can't love football and live abroad because you miss the one thing you want to watch – your team. **"**

The EnD

" Don't send me flowers when I'm dead. If you like me,
send them while I'm alive. "

After the liver transplant which saved his life.